Generating a Lasting Legacy

8 Lessons to Teach Your Children

Mark Queen

Generating a Lasting Legacy

Published by:
90-Minute Books
302 Martinique Drive
Winter Haven, FL 33884
www.90minutebooks.com

Published in the United States of America

ISBN-13: 978-0692570968
ISBN-10: 0692570969

For more information on 90-Minute Books including finding out how you can publish your own lead generating book, visit www.90minutebooks.com or call (863) 318-0464

Here's What's Inside...

Introduction

I was just concluding a client meeting and, as my clients stood up to leave, they mentioned that they were preparing to go on a family vacation. The couple, who have several adult children and teenagers still at home, asked me to suggest a single lesson they could focus on while talking with their adult children and teenagers while on vacation. I was awestruck and immediately apologized to them because I realized there are many life lessons my clients have taught me which I might have been sharing with my other clients.

We're all concerned about the next generation. We want them to be better off than we are. We want them to be better off financially, societally, in their relationships, in their businesses and in how they live their lives. We really want them to be even better assets to the society in which they perform and function.

I personally believe that, in our society, the problems we face today are not going to be solved through large groups getting together and having large discussions to find large solutions to large problems. I believe our large problems are actually going to be solved on a microscopic scale, as individuals begin to take the responsibility of providing value in their own lives. To do that, we want to try to make sure the next generation is better off. For the next generation to be better off, we have to start providing them with lessons and guidance rather than continuing in the haphazard manner of past generations. Our passing these lessons on to the next generations seems to have been lost somewhat.

As I went about shaping the material, I realized that our education system is creating instruction that's designed for the masses. It really educates people to just the average. I realize that this may not be a popular statement but this book isn't being written for the sake of popularity. It's written for the benefit of the future of our families. Our families need to support our individual family members as they work to experience above average generational success. If that's going to happen, we can't count on society's normal education methods. As leaders and heads of families, we have to take that ball ourselves, we need to take control of it, and we need to lead and teach them ourselves.

So here's some lessons that you might find valuable and that I've shared with my children.

Mark Queen

Generating a Lasting Legacy

I want to acknowledge the parents who are reading this who both know their families' core values and take the time to share these with their children. I know quite a few elite families out there who have been teaching generational lessons to their younger family members as they grow up. Unfortunately, that's not the norm and those who do it know it takes leadership. In the United States, a fairly young country in the world, we are strong believers in capitalism. In our capitalistic society, it's not uncommon for an entrepreneur to create something in his or her own life which the previous generations have never created before. Most entrepreneurs aren't running companies which have been handed down to them; most entrepreneurs are creating successful enterprises from the ground up.

Often, entrepreneurial success comes from a great deal of hard work, as well as a lot of trial and error. There is no road map to follow. Yes, you might see a business plan put together but that plan doesn't implement all the steps or take actions or make decisions for the entrepreneur. The entrepreneur must find the path to success. They have to take those actions and make those decisions to run their companies. We've learned from our success in teaching important life lessons to our own children that they need that same level of leadership at home to lead their families in their success. Family success might be more than just the result of a series of trial-and-error events. With strong leadership we can transform those lessons, so they are really an exponential growth factor compounding throughout their lives with their families. If they do this, they will have continual family growth, without that individual experience of repeating the same setbacks again and again.

You see, whether someone knows it or not, most people have a set of core values. If you were to ask them what values they believe in or what values they have in their life, they might be able to elicit a few values or beliefs but rarely are they written down. By being very specific and dedicated to a process, you can actually develop and create a core set of values that you can share with your family members. You can then be supportive of those family members, without judgment, and help them learn and live life exponentially. When this happens, it creates a positive collaborative environment.

With a little bit of training, we can leave behind some of those judgment filters which allow us to blame people. As heads of households, we're really looking to make a positive investment in our future so that our families can continue to grow. That's my definition of success for a family. If we can provide our families with a set of core values which we can propagate throughout the generations, our families will be able to subscribe to those core values, perhaps amend them and help grow that core value set over time. We want to help families develop their core values and share them regularly with their children so their children can grow up and do the same for their children. This then provides a lasting legacy which transcends generations.

When sharing those values, it can be done in many different ways. We know that many societies shared things orally. I like to think of the old west and settler's families telling stories of old around a camp fire, in the Heartland of America. We can, however, share other ways as well.

We live in a very technological age. Digital and electronic media are advancing almost daily. The speed of the computer chip is said to double about every 2 years. What will technology bring in the next five, ten or twenty years and how will your family use it to share your values? We know that if you don't start capturing those values somehow, they might not get captured at all.

8 Lessons to Teach Your Children

Lesson One: There's Always Something Bigger than One's Self

As I sat down to come up with the lessons I've taught my children, the very first one that gripped me was that most successful people and most families believe that there's always something bigger than one's self. It may be your faith, your understanding that a family is comprised of more than one individual, your knowledge that there's power in the concept of the team and that we can act as a team when we're acting as a family. There doesn't always have to be sibling rivalry. If there is, we can grow out of it as we learn that there is something bigger than ourselves.

When we recognize that we can be a part of something bigger, by acting as a team, we have the ability to grow through accountability to one another. We begin to see the importance of collaborative efforts and how we can successfully use each person's unique sets of skills and talents. By partnering these individuals and their skills and talents with others, it is possible for you to experience exponential growth. The exponential power of two is not addition. One plus one does not equal two when it comes to being part of a powerful team.

There are numerous sports analogies that apply here but let's consider baseball. In baseball, you have nine players on the field because you're not going to win many ballgames with just a pitcher and a catcher. It's not every day that a pitcher and a catcher are going to strike out every batter in a game. A single hit would cause failure and a run would score. When collaborating on a baseball field, we need all nine players to be present on the team. Can you imagine what might happen if a baseball team with 14 players were allowed to play against a team with nine? If I were a gambling person, I would bet on the team with 14 players on the field.

It is important to understand that you can provide more value as part of a team versus doing it by yourself. Just because you're an individual, it doesn't mean you have to do everything by yourself. Team up and work collaboratively.

Lesson Two: We Must Take Risks

Lesson number two has to do with risks. It seems in our society that it's common for people not to want to take risks. Risks are seen as something dangerous, something to be avoided. I don't believe this is necessarily true. I believe you have to take risks. If you're not taking risks, the likelihood of failure may be reduced, but the likelihood of outstanding success is reduced as well, maybe to an even greater degree.

I believe that to achieve is to actually survive failing and to fail is to achieve. Successful families and individuals figure out ways to mitigate the costs of failure. In our family, we encourage people to take risks, to talk about them, to find ways to mitigate them but we don't encourage satisfaction with the status quo. Regardless of what part of your life you're in, you need to look for risks.

When it comes to your relationships, you need to grow. You're not going to find deep and meaningful relationships by holing up in a basement apartment playing video games. There's not much risk to leading a life like that. To grow financially, you're going to have to take some risks. Are you going to take some money out of your checking account, put it in a savings account, and take the risk that you won't spend it next week?

If you're not going to take risks inside of your faith and look around at other faiths, you're not going to understand what other people believe. How do we compare what we might believe to be an appropriate answer in relation to what we call our creator with what someone else believes if we won't take a risk?

I don't know many businesses that aren't taking risks. Most businesses employ people, and if you employ people, you are always going to be dealing with risk. That's part of what people bring to your organization. We can train our people, send them to continuing education, send them for more schooling and invest in them continually, however, we can't control people's behaviors. When people act on your behalf, you're putting yourself at risk by allowing others to represent you.

We have already learned that we have to believe in a team spirit, that we've got to be part of a bigger story. So, when we bring other people in, we know that's going to bring in a level of risk. When hiring, we look for the right person for the right position. We don't knowingly hire the wrong person for any position.

Successful families simply figure out how to mitigate those risks. In our family we mitigate these risks by encouraging taking healthy risks.

There are lots of ways to mitigate risks but that's the how part of life. This book isn't about the how's it's about the why's. Core Values are almost always about why we do things.

Lesson Three: Create New Habits throughout Your Life

As human beings, we are creatures of habit. We like to find the most comfortable way to complete a task. It's even been proven in research that our brains work in this way. We actually create pathways in our brains that help us to mitigate the amount of energy we use when we make a decision. This is the brain's habit pattern.

The challenge is that if our brains are always trying to find ways to use the least amount of energy and create habits from that, whatever habits we have in play today are only going to take us to what I call a habit plateau. We can only be so successful with our current repertoire of habits.

If we would like to achieve a higher level of success, I think it is common sense to think we've got to have a different set of habits. Each individual family will decide what those habits are depending on what they're trying to achieve. What we have to learn as individuals is that if we want to have a higher level of success throughout our lifetimes, we have to learn how to create new habits.

Generationally successful families always encourage the development of new, healthy habits and they've always been supportive of individuals as they create these new habits. While the person may have one outcome in mind when they set out to create a new habit, that doesn't mean that the newly created habit is what they originally intended. Often, we arrive at a result and find that it indeed was not the result that we desired. So, even though you might have a new habit, you also have to learn that it's okay to get rid of an old habit when the new one is inserted. Successful families encourage their members to continue to do this throughout their lives.

It's easy to identify that my habits as a young, unmarried individual were focused on finding a significant other in my life. Once I found a significant other however, I had a different set of habits. Specifically, my habits changed to ones that I would need as I began to raise a family. When we had an infant around the house, there had better be some new habits developed, or we're going to have an infant who wasn't going to be very happy or clean. Without those new habits the baby wasn't going to be clean, fed or provided with the love and attention needed to thrive.

I'm not just talking about my or other parents' habits. Everybody needs to continue to build on their habits throughout life. Parents have to subscribe to this and create new habits for themselves to raise an infant. At the same time, the brand new grandfathers and grandmothers are going to have to develop new habits in their lives. They're going to have to figure out how to hold that infant and enjoy having a grandchild in their lives.

Financially, the individual who is just beginning to build a savings account is going to develop a different set of habits, and at a different level, then someone who already has a significant net worth.

There are many conflicting numbers around how long it takes to develop a new habit but for arguments sake lets agree to use 21 days as how long it takes to develop a new habit. If we can change a habit every 21 days, then we know that we can change many habits throughout a year. In fact, creating a new habit can have exponential results. Think about someone who decides to create a habit of waking up 30 minutes earlier for the rest of their life. When will breakfast, lunch and dinner occur in the future? Those are all likely to change. Will the old bedtime routine stay the same? What will happen to the energy level through the day and what will the person do with the extra 30 minutes?

The development of new habits gives us the ability to put priorities on what we believe is most important and take actions accordingly. No one needs to be excluded from learning new habits. Everybody in the family, regardless of age, can benefit and learn by building new habits.

Lesson Four: Be a Lifetime Student—Never Stop Learning

We must be students of lifetime learning. I think there's a common perception that education starts with elementary school. Once you're done with elementary school, you go on to secondary school. We have set, as a societal standard, to expect everyone to make it through high school. Then, if you want to pursue higher levels of education, you go to college. Then, once you get through college, whether it's a bachelor's degree, graduate degree, or doctorate, that phase of learning is done.

The fact is public education is only the first segment in a lifetime of education. When we complete that public education, the lessons of life really begin to be seen. Our focus isn't on a grade anymore but on experiencing life. There are lessons of life we learn through relationships, whether they're through professional relationships, through our faith, through our neighbors, or through our social environment. We learn financial lessons as our finances change over time.

So, when we begin to look at the different elements of life as being personal, financial, entrepreneurial, and social, we might say, "I'm probably going to change throughout those times." As we change, we are offered opportunities to learn. Even though you're not attending a university, public school, or private school, it doesn't mean that once you're done with those institutions, you're done with learning. We need to keep our eyes open and our minds awake, so we are ready to learn on a continuing basis.

One of the best ways to pass this lesson on to our children is to model learning. You can do that by always encouraging them to ask questions. A question requires somebody to actually develop a brain pattern, or a thought pattern, to respond to the question. Good questions are designed to avoid passing judgment. Good questions, without judgment, will actually lead to a conversation, during which ideas can be exchanged.

As an example, you could ask, "Which of those restaurants do you believe is more profitable?" I'm not judging either one of those restaurants. I'm not making a decision of which one we should eat at. By asking that question, I've been able to begin to have a conversation and to listen to the participants as they express their thoughts so we can exchange ideas.

As we continue to explore our world by asking questions, we can continue the process of learning. When do we run out of questions? We should never run out of questions.

The distinction here is that rather than trying to teach and advise our children, we should instead instill in them a sense of curiosity, which will serve them much longer than having to depend on others for the answers. You're gifting them with a mindset of lifetime learning.

It's been said that if we're not growing, we're decaying. Some people like to say if we're not growing, we're dying; there's no in-between. If we stop learning when we finish school, then our learning is in decay. We're actually regressing. We don't need a bunch of scientific information to tell us that, all we have to do is ask anybody who has a child. Ask anybody in education about a student's aptitude at the start of a new school year according to where the student was at the end of the year, before the summer break. It's not uncommon for a student to backslide a little bit in relation to where he or she left off in their studies. Now, the child may be able to pick it right up relatively quickly but it takes some reminders to make progress.

I hope that in our family, our core set of values says, "Let's be lifetime learners. Let's backslide as little as possible." Let our lifetime learning be a catalyst of exponential family growth instead of having to make individual corrections all the time. Backsliding wouldn't be addition in mathematics, it would be subtraction. Our goal should be to replace backsliding with exponential growth shifts.

Lesson Five: The Largest Threats to Long-Term Financial Success Are Our Spending and Saving Habits

The fifth lesson is the largest financial threat to one's long term success, one's spending and saving habits. Our educational system doesn't teach much about the subject of personal finances. I certainly didn't get much. I've met some people in our public education system who teach the very basics of financial lessons, such as budgeting, for example. Basically, the lessons are simple though, you must save some money for yourself.

Our society as a whole though is about spending. So why would our educational system, as established by our society, reflect anything different. When people live beyond their means, they are living in the future financially. We don't have time machines so this theory doesn't work in the long run. We need to be selective about how we set up our habits in this regard.

For most people of faith, the first priority is to give towards their faith. Then, they might save some money for themselves, to provide for the future. After that, they go out and spend what's left. Societies across the world show that those with greater amounts of disposable income are presented with constant input regarding a wide variety of products which will take up the major portion of their spare cash. The number of available products is greater today than ever. This is especially true in a capitalistic society, particularly in the successful United States and Western Hemisphere. Those who have that discretionary income have to learn how to put some back.

You might have heard statistics that indicate approximately 50 percent of the so-called windfall winners are actually worse off financially after they receive their windfall. This group includes professional athletes, who all of a sudden have signed large contracts; and lottery winners, who suddenly have millions of dollars or hundreds of thousands of dollars to deal with on an annual basis. To reiterate. About fifty percent of those people are in worse financial circumstances after their windfall.

How can that be? The theory is they don't have good habits in place which are necessary to manage their windfall. It's imperative to be able to get on top of creating good spending and saving habits. The sooner you start, the better off you're going to be. Regardless of what level of success you're going to have professionally or financially, it takes a good start with the habit of saving first and spending second.

I can't think of a more powerful lesson to instill in your children, or one that will have a greater impact on their long-term success than their spending and saving habits.

Lesson Six: There Are Both People and Capital at Work. Work Both.

Lesson number six is, there are people at work and there is your capital at work. The key for generational success is to work both. What do I mean by that? Not many people are blessed with a large windfall from their families, not many people are blessed with the windfall of being a professional athlete, and not many people are blessed by winning the lottery. Once you've accumulated some capital, because you have saved more than you have spent, the goal is to have that capital go to work for you. We want the capital to be working while you are doing something else.

Everyone would like to have their own legal printing press that would spit out 20-dollar bills whenever it was turned on. If you had this kind of money machine, how often would you put that machine to work? There would never be a reason to shut the machine down, right? Well, that's exactly what we are trying to do when we are putting our capital to work. If we build and invest our capital with that in mind, it's as if it's working for us all the time.

At the same time, if you had that money machine, who would oil it, take care of its preventative maintenance, run the necessary software? Who's going to plug it in, turn it on, and make sure that it runs properly when you're away on vacation? That takes human capital, an actual person.

If you haven't had a large windfall or you lack capital that's working for you, it's your responsibility to go to work. You must be the person who's going to receive a paycheck, an income of some kind, so you have the ability to provide for yourself, to accumulate some capital and let it go to work for you. And if you instill in yourself the self-worth and the self-identity to say, "I am productive in what I can do," at no point in your future will you ever have to stop being productive. Personally, I despise the word retire. I don't know why anybody pursuing a passion which has helped fulfill his or her mission in life of providing value to themselves and to others would ever choose to stop doing that. With the health and capability needed to do it, why would anyone ever want to stop working?

This supports our family's concept that you need to be working as a person and to have your capital working. People need to work to provide value to others and to receive the rewards of compensation and increased self-worth. By either earning a wage or tapping into the profitability of an organization or company, we may be able to generate excess capital which isn't needed for the vital purposes of living and we have the option to put this capital to work for us. Our family believes that to be successful and have exponential generational growth, we must always provide value to others—provide the work and work the capital.

Kids today see people who have made the choice to not be productive. It happens in the United States and across the globe. They see it on their sports teams. People come in and they want to participate on the athletic team but they're not willing to work, to put in the practice, to put in the hours. Kids see people in their schools who don't take school seriously. They don't do the hours of homework required to move ahead in our school systems. They see people right beside them who aren't being productive. They are totally capable both physically and mentally to be productive in our society, providing value somehow, but they've chosen not to for some reason. I think there are probably examples of this in every city.

From a young age, we have taught our children to recognize that they need to contribute on both sides of the equation—work and capital. This lesson will probably be with us as long as people walk the earth.

Lesson Seven: Liquidity Is a Requirement

Liquidity is a requirement. What do I mean by liquidity? Liquidity means that I'm keeping some capital in my life, where I can get my hands on it. So, when I need to do something, first and foremost, I don't need to ask somebody else's permission to be able to do it. We see many examples in our life where people have been able to make money on a capital transaction of some kind. People have been able to buy an asset, whether it is a toy or a piece of capital like a home or a car, something that has value in their lives. If you don't have the capital to take advantage of it, then opportunities will be missed. So, we need to keep some of our capital liquid to take advantage of the opportunities that come to us, not at the expense of other people, but because of situational environments.

Recently, my truck developed a serious problem. The frame rusted out. To me, that vehicle no longer represented a safe vehicle to drive, it had become virtually worthless. I had no trust in it as a mode of transportation. I could not trust it to move me from point A to point B. For me, the value of that vehicle was zero. However, it did have a perfectly functional, modern transmission, a nice set of tires and a topper that was in good condition. I wound up selling that vehicle for much more than I ever thought I would because somebody else needed that model transmission. We struck a deal and the gentleman who bought the truck handed me some hundred-dollar bills to pay for it. There were plenty of people who could have gone to the bank to withdraw money to purchase that truck.

That individual was a great example of someone who was able to take advantage of an opportunity. I was willing to sell the vehicle at a bargain basement price to him because he could make use of it. I was happy to make the transaction. This type of opportunity presents itself all the time. We have to be ready and we have to be liquid.

Your liquidity today might be comfortable but that doesn't mean it will be tomorrow. Liquidity changes. Needs related to liquidity change throughout life. Just as an individual's standard of living will in all probability increase, their liquidity needs will probably increase as well. As we prepare for more and greater opportunities and gain the ability to take advantage of more opportunities, it seems that more actually seem to present themselves so you'll need greater and greater liquidity. So, as liquidity shifts throughout your life, you need to be able to manage that process and transformation.

Lesson Eight: Diversification Can Be a Friend and an Enemy

We often hear the old saying, "Don't put all your eggs in one basket." This quote speaks to the value of diversification—how we should spread ourselves around. The fact is, I believe that diversification is your friend but it can also be your enemy. What do I mean by that? When we think about our liquidity, for example, let's assume that you think that you might need standard liquidity. Is it really necessary to have standard liquidity stuffed under your mattress or hidden in your garden? Maybe some goes in a savings account, maybe some goes in a checking account, maybe it goes into ten different savings accounts. I'm not quite sure the level of diversification achieved by spreading it out so thin is actually effective though. It actually costs us time to go gather up all of our liquidity if we are spread too thin. It takes energy and resources to go out and retrieve all of that liquidity if it's spread too thin. Even in this digital age and with the power of the Internet, if your accounts are all online, even though they might be successfully diversified among so many different accounts, is that effective if the Internet crashes?

With diversification, we can be spread too thin. I don't want to limit our thoughts by saying that diversification only applies to our finances because it's broader than that. It is possible to have more than one relationship. I heard from the platform at a million-dollar round table that it's possible to have 12 of the deepest human relationships possible at a time. Now, we can have many, many more relationships than that at any given moment but of the deepest human relationships, our minds and hearts only have the capacity to accommodate twelve. Isn't that interesting? It's only 12. Why isn't it 24? I believe it's because, when you begin to think about what a relationship requires, including time, energy, and resources, how could you possibly have and sustain a deep personal relationship if you're trying to do it with 50 different people? How would you be in contact with them every day, every week, or every month? So, depending on what your definition is of a deep personal relationship, you have to understand you can't be in a deep personal relationship with 200 people. It's going to be restrictive.

Diversification is powerful. Do I like the fact that I can have 12 different relationships at the deepest human level? I absolutely do, because I enjoy many different things. Not all my friends enjoy all of the same things that I do but I like finding one or two to spend time with. For example, I enjoy doing different things with my friend, Greg, than I enjoy with my friend, Phil. My wife and I enjoy doing different things than I enjoy with my two sons or my daughter.

Diversification is your friend and it can be your enemy. The key that we've learned is that we need to set strategies for ourselves related to maintaining the appropriate level of diversification, whether it's your finances, relationships, or any other aspect of your life. Then, after you've set your strategy, you need to be tactical and know specifically what you're going to do. I can tell you that in my relationship with my wife, I want to be diversified with her. I want to be sure that I'm setting a strategy for saying, "Honey, we're going to have a date every week," and we do that. However, being tactical doesn't mean that we do the same things every week. Our strategy says, "Make sure that we go out on a date night and enjoy an activity together." Tactically, that could be dinner out, joining friends, playing cards, enjoying a game night or it may be that we see a movie together. We certainly don't want to get spread too thin though.

Why Keeping Score Leads a Family toward Exponential Growth

As you continue to introduce these life lessons to your children, keep in mind that what you measure changes. So, wherever in life we want to have a higher level of success, we want to begin to teach our children the lessons we find to be central to our family. The first thing to do is to begin to set up a system to measure whether or not you're being successful because when you begin to measure something, your behavior will change to satisfy a minimum-level objective for your goal. For example, a family who wants to set a level of core values for themselves and wants to be sure to discuss it with their family might actually sit down and decide that every time they take a family vacation, they were going to make sure to discuss one of the family's core values. This serves as a standard which would happen regardless of where the family goes on vacation or what activities they participate in.

Imagine a child who from age seven goes on family vacations and listens to discussions about family core values year after year. By the time he graduates from high school, he will certainly know his family's core values, won't he? Most likely, he'll be aware of more than eight, although many families don't achieve that because they don't measure. They leave their values to be learned via haphazard methods. If the children pick up on it, even without our intention and focus, then so be it. That's not how we want to drive our families successfully for generational growth. What is the definition of successful growth? I guess it depends on our means of measurement?

At the end of a football game, or any sports endeavor, there generally is a scoreboard where the time clock ticks down. Eventually, the timer hits zero, a buzzer goes off, bells and whistles blow, and people celebrate the score. Why do they celebrate the score? Because, there's a measurement there. The only reason you're keeping score is to have a measurement that defines what success is.

There are many different levels of success. Right now, as I write this book, we're in the middle of baseball season. People are keeping score so they'll know how they did. Who won today's game. But in a wider realm, they're keeping that score to know who's won the game so they can get to the end of the season and determine which teams go on to the playoffs. Then, at the end of the season only the teams that accumulate the most wins will make it to the playoffs. That's not the end of it though. We now find that once you get to the playoffs, you tally up those wins and the top teams advance to a division championship. The division championships are followed by the World Series. The entire endeavor is a series of measurements.

As a family, when we have the ability to identify our core values, we can then begin to have very easy, open conversations to determine how we should keep score. If you can keep score, you can eventually lead your family towards exponential growth and at that point, win a World Series for family success.

How to Talk to Your Children about Core Family Values

The first step is to identify your family core values so you're able to talk about them with clarity. You can then practice communicating and polishing them with others. Maybe that's someone at work or a professional like myself until you can state them well yourself and understand the depth to which they really apply to your family's success. When you have a thorough understanding, it's much easier to begin to have conversations about them with your children.

We also want to find ways in which the lessons can be related to and understood by the kids. In our family, it's very easy for us to talk about the team concept as our family is active in sports and in our faith. We've participated in numerous activities as a family all over the world.

I have an interesting story to prove this out. We traveled to St. Louis, Missouri to see a Kansas State football game. As I remember, it may have been the very first Big 12 Championship Game against Texas A&M. We took all three of our children to that ballgame and after we checked in at our hotel upon arrival in St. Louis, we caught the elevator to go upstairs to our rooms. As we did, my daughter who I think was probably around four years old at the time, was anxious to be first one on the elevator. My son Brian was probably six or seven at the time and he had pushed the button to bring the elevator to the first floor. Kristen, our little Kristen, ran into the elevator and hit a button which closed the door without anybody else being on the elevator. Well, if you can imagine, there was a little bit of panic that set in. We were quickly able to divide up as a family to be able to figure out how we were going to be able to find where Kristen was in a strange city and a strange hotel. We had a lost family member, and a little one, at that.

We were able to station our oldest son at that elevator door. We told him to stay there, to not move. As soon as he could find an adult, he would tell them what was going on and asked them to stay there with him. Then, of course, the rest of us scattered. My wife headed to the main floor while I headed to the upper floors. When my wife got to the main floor, she saw that the elevator which our daughter was on, thankfully, had gone there and that all was fine. She realized that when the elevator got to the main floor our daughter must have walked out, a security guard must have seen her, walked over to her and stayed with her until my wife arrived.

From that event, we learned that if just one person had run through that hotel trying to find a little toddler, we would not have had the same level of confidence we had because we had been able to put together a good plan of action which led to a positive resolution. If you were to ask my children today whether or not they learned anything from that day, I think all three would tell you yes, they learned something. I don't think anyone can say there's a cut-off age for learning. As a parent, you simply need to know what you want to convey to your kids and then be able to communicate it to them.

How to Generate a Lasting Legacy

My hope is that somebody will read this book and say, "Mark, the lessons you've taught your family, your family's core values resonate with me and my family. Maybe it's time for me to do a better job of communicating with my family about them." If I've inspired you, I will consider taking on the project of writing this book to be a success.

If anybody needs help within their entrepreneurial family to help shape and create a system in which they can measure and create a set of core values, I'd be happy to have a conversation with you about how to shape that set of values. Just because you're an individual family, just because you're the leader of a family does not mean you have to do everything by yourself. My companies and the teams I lead believe in that and it's one of our team's core values.

I'd love to talk with you in person to answer any questions you have about how to use these principles as a source of learning and growth for future generations. To learn more, please visit www.MarkQueen.info.

Here's How to Generate a Lasting Legacy by Teaching Your Family's Core Values

I'll bet that you remember stories from your life where the values that you live by were formed. There are stories of joy and of sorrow, of standing tall and standing your ground. There are stories about the people that taught you and shaped you. You probably recall financial lessons, lessons about work or lack of it, and lessons about strength of character and the lessons of times of weakness of character, but what most people don't have is a means to transfer those values. You can have a great set of legal and financial advisors that you work with and never create any kind of transfer plan that's focused on sharing your core values. It's not the education system's responsibility to Teach Your Family your Core Values.

You already know today's modern world is moving faster and is more complicated than when you were a kid. Technology is changing how our families relate, how we learn and what we learn. What we gain in confidence through technology might challenge us when creating confidence about our values. A confusing part of the values transfer process is not knowing how to pass along your family's core values to your kids and grandchildren.

That's where we come in. We help people just like you leave a lasting legacy by sharing your family's core values. We can help your team understand how to strengthen the transfer process. For some, they realize that their planning has been too short sighted because it wasn't based on the core values of the family. If you are transferring your wealth without sharing how your values shaped the process, I suspect that the transition isn't going to go the way you would really prefer. That's where we can help.

We can...

Step 1: Identify your family core values so you're able to talk about them with clarity.

Step 2: Identify ways in which your core values can be related to and understood by the kids.

Step 3: Create opportunities to discuss and share your core values with your kids so the sharing of your core values becomes part of the family environment. We can help you share your full vision with your team of advisors to make a truly effective transition plan.

Most people don't stop and identify the core values they want to pass along from generation to generation. They settle for a set of legal documents which takes care of your wealth but not the core of your heart.

Now, you can identify and teach your kids the core values that will set them up for success for generations to come.

If you'd like us to help, just send an email to: info@MarkQueen.info and we will take it from there.

Made in the USA
Monee, IL
04 November 2026

67386100R00020